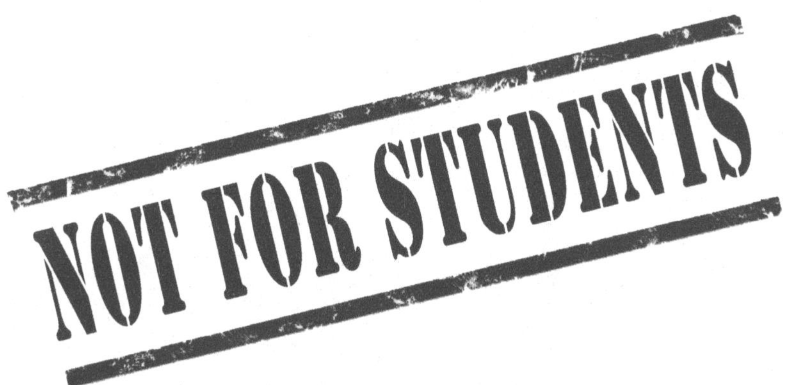

Tamara Michael

Not For Students By Tamara Michael

Published by Archibald Press

© 2021 Tamara Michael

ISBN: 978-0-6451822-1-7

Disclaimer

You know those teachers who live and breathe to teach? They have the most beautiful room and the most amazing lessons? Their eyes sparkle when they talk about their students, and they spend hours working on their lesson plans? Yeah, this book is not for them.

This book is for the teachers doing their best, and getting by one day at a time.

I am you.

Acknowledgements

I'd like to thank the students who almost made me want to quit. You made me better in every way.

I'd also like to thank my brother Salim and sister Sarah who usually like my ideas.

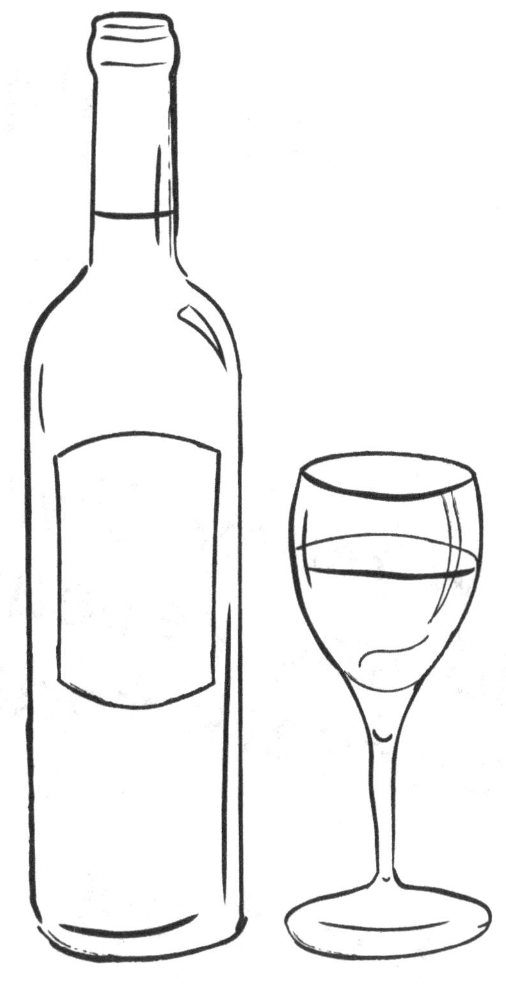

Grab a drink babe,
you know you need it!

How many times
did you repeat
yourself today?

Tally it up!

WHO FARTED
IN YOUR
CLASSROOM
TODAY?

Imagine you called in sick today, what would you do with your day?

WRITE A LIST OF
MOVIES THAT *SEEM*
EDUCATIONAL BUT
REALLY AREN'T.

List all the things you
need to survive a
wet weather day.

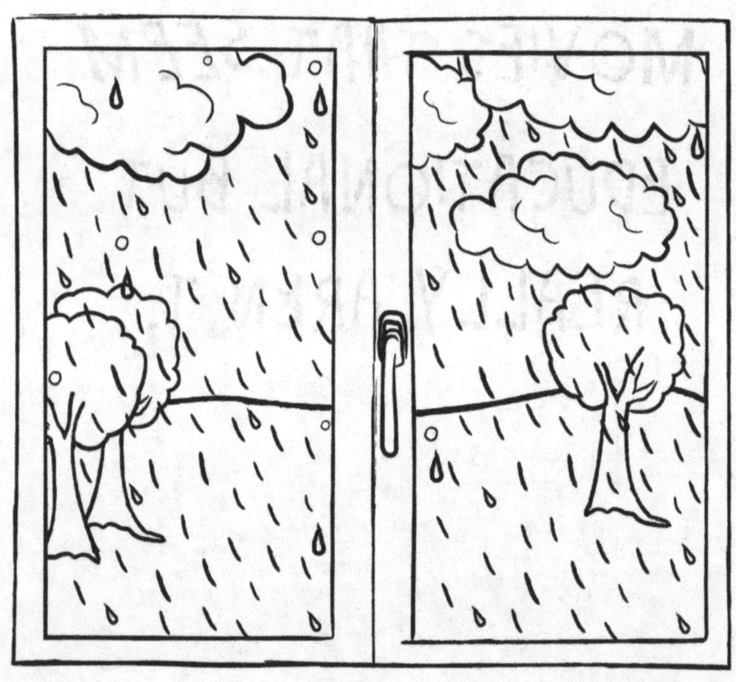

For example, bucketloads of coffee.

If a robot took over your job, what would you do with all your free time?

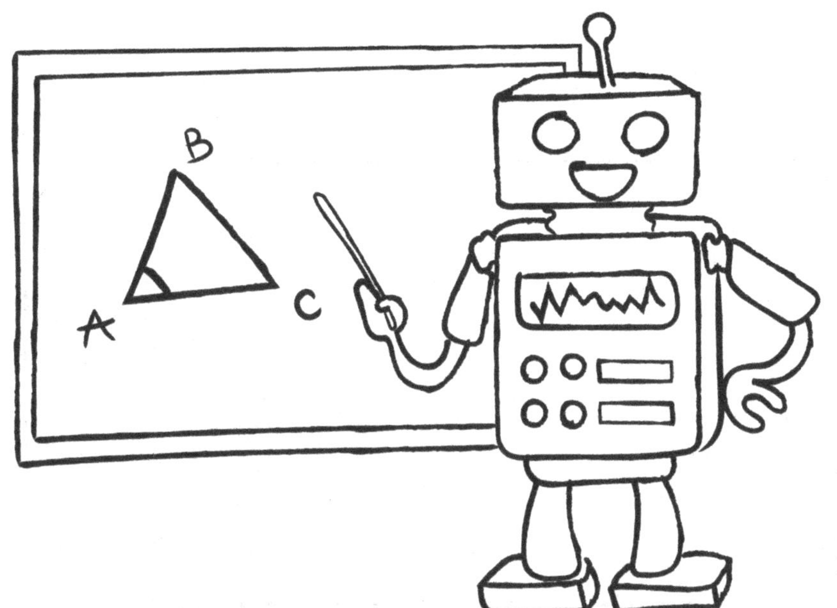
B
A
C

DRAW A SELF-PORTRAIT
OF YOU ON THE
LAST DAY OF SCHOOL.

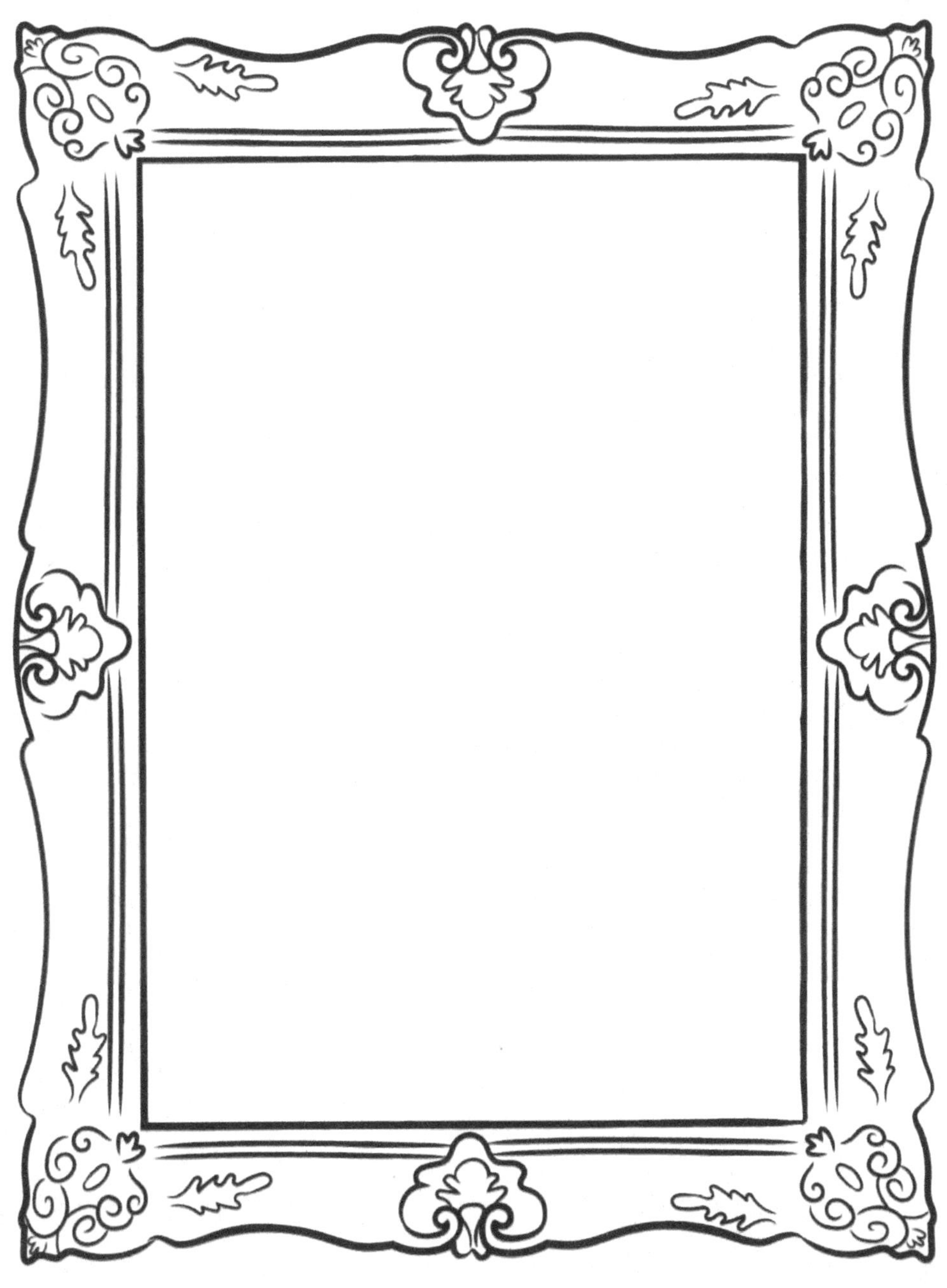

Write out a list
of things you wish
you could say at
parent-teacher
night.

Take out all your frustration on these pages.

Describe your
dream job.

List all the things you wish you could say to kids when they push your buttons.

How early is too early to let them out for lunch?

Complete this sentence.

SCHOOL IS. . .

CIRCLE

TWO TRUTHS

AND A LIE.

I am not underpaid.

I love every student.

I have spent too much of
my own money on resources.

I have dreams about my
classroom.

I love extra playground duty.

school assemblies are so fun.

ASSIGN THESE CLASS AWARDS TO THE MOST DESERVING STUDENTS

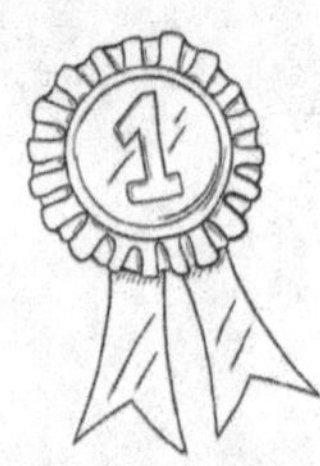 **M**ost likely to get arrested.

____

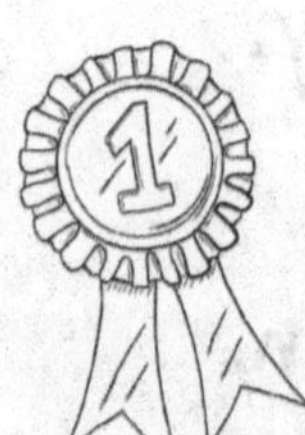 **M**ost likely to become a millionaire.

____

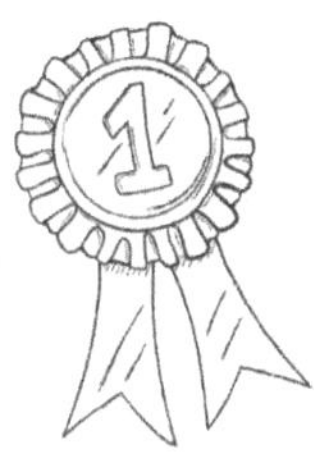 Most likely to become famous.

 Most likely to become a teacher.

WRITE OUT ALL THE THINGS YOU GET DONE IN A FIFTEEN MINUTE LUNCH BREAK.

When you were a child, what did you want to be when you grew up?

Sip and Search

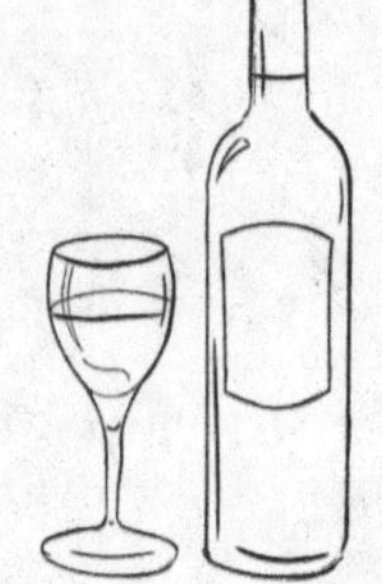

```
O  I  I  E  E  C  V  L  E  H  L  Y  U  S
P  I  N  O  T  G  R  I  G  I  O  M  R  A
P  E  U  P  C  A  B  E  R  N  E  T  N  X
S  A  U  V  I  G  N  O  N  B  L  A  N  C
R  B  P  A  R  N  B  I  A  X  I  O  S  T
M  E  R  L  O  T  O  S  F  F  P  E  H  B
T  L  D  R  G  I  K  T  S  H  I  R  A  Z
X  S  O  V  U  F  C  J  N  Z  U  E  A  W
R  O  S  E  C  H  A  R  D  O  N  N  A  Y
C  H  A  M  P  A  G  N  E  A  I  O  E  T
O  G  M  A  L  B  E  C  N  G  K  R  F  T
E  Y  Z  E  X  I  N  F  M  X  P  S  I  D
D  E  K  A  K  M  D  Q  F  E  O  E  I  E
```

Pinot Noir

Champagne

Cabernet

Shiraz

Chardonnay

Sauvignon Blanc

Pinot Grigio

Merlot

Rosé

Malbec

Write a letter to
your eighteen-
year-old self.

If you were principal for a day, what would you change?

List three things you have to teach that you actually think are BS.

Don't think, just draw the first thing that pops into your mind.

Turn the squiggles below
into an image.

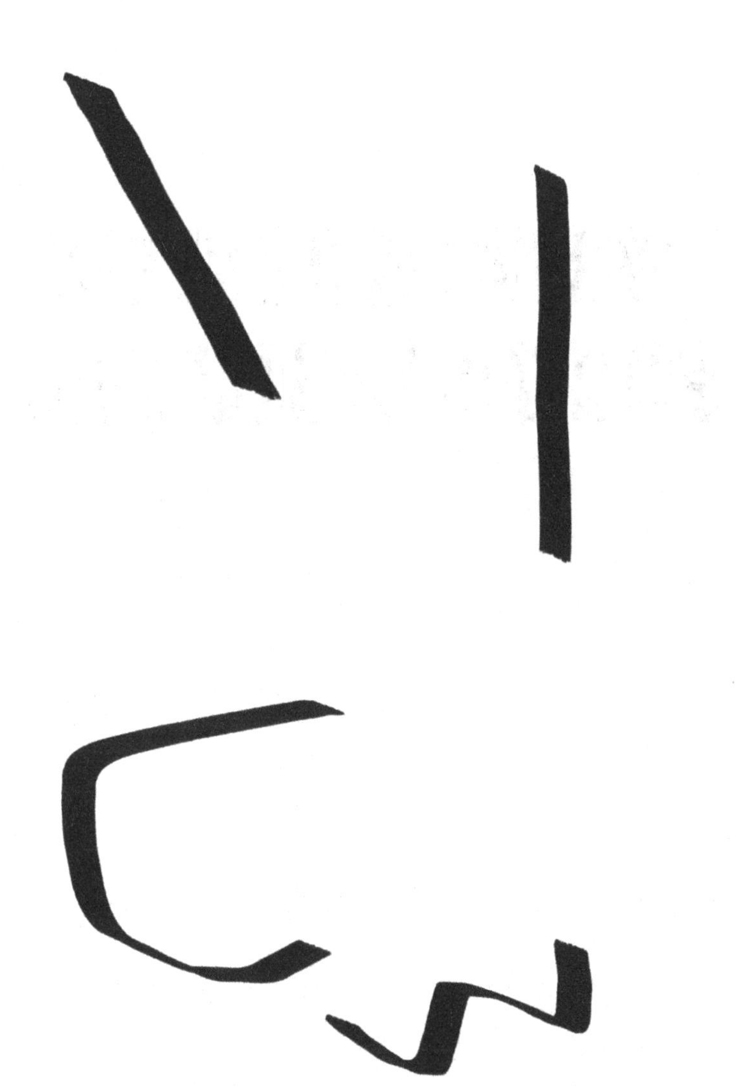

WRITE A REVIEW FOR YOUR SCHOOL.

circle all the statements that apply to you until you get three in a row.

I showed up to school hungover.	I didn't have a lesson plan all day.	Ignored a student on purpose.
I played a movie because I couldn't be bothered to teach.	I secretly can't stand the teacher's pet.	I googled other jobs I can do with a teaching degree.
I let kids out to lunch super early because I needed a break.	I hate my "teacher" voice.	I hid in my classroom to avoid small talk in the staff room.

Write about a great thing that happened today.

Draw a bad thing that
happened today.

Draw all the things you would pack in your bag in order to survive the first day back at school.

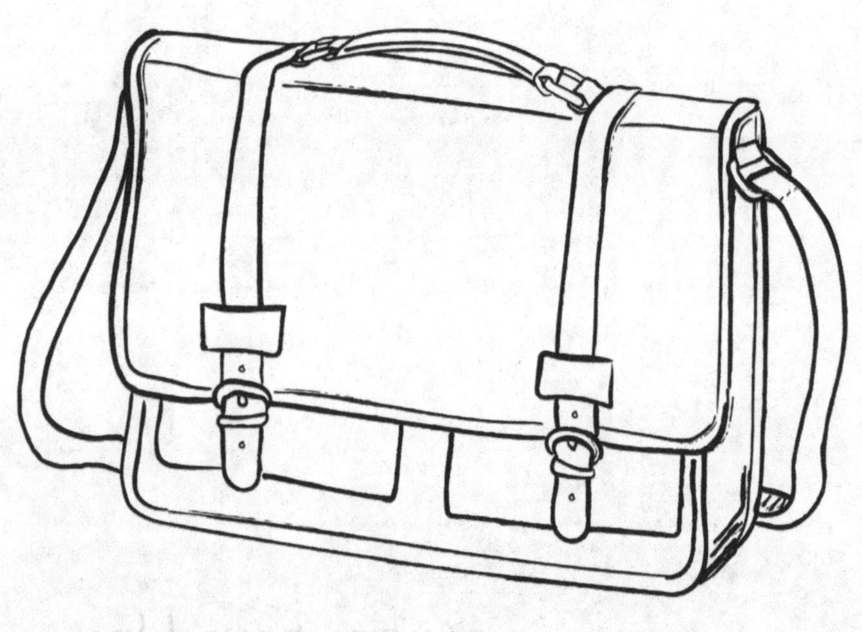

DRAW YOUR LEAST FAVOURITE STUDENT AS AN UNDISCOVERED CREATURE FROM THE DEPTHS OF THE OCEAN.

List or label all its features and abilities.

A TEACHER'S DRINKING GAME.

TALLY EVERY TIME YOU HEAR THE WORD "MISS" OR "SIR" TODAY. FOR EACH TALLY MARK, TAKE ONE SHOT! (NOT AT SCHOOL, OBVIOUSLY).

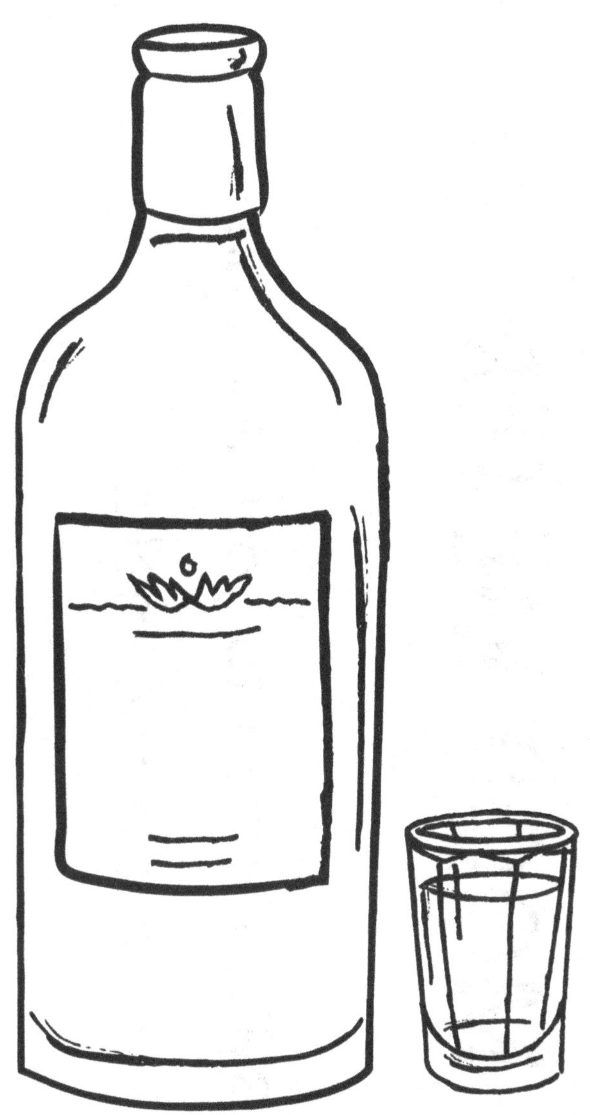

MOOD METER

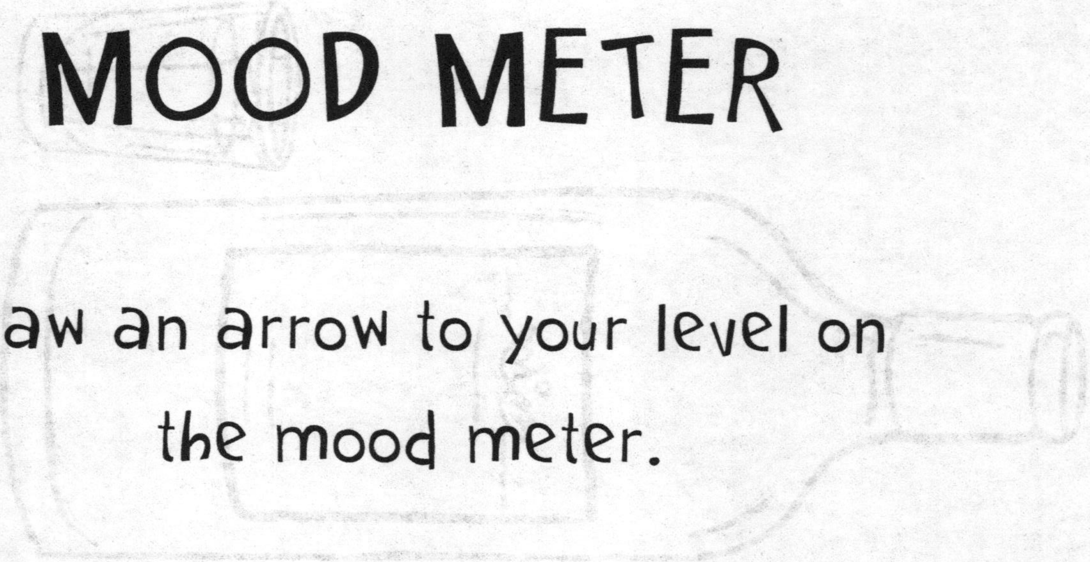

Draw an arrow to your level on the mood meter.

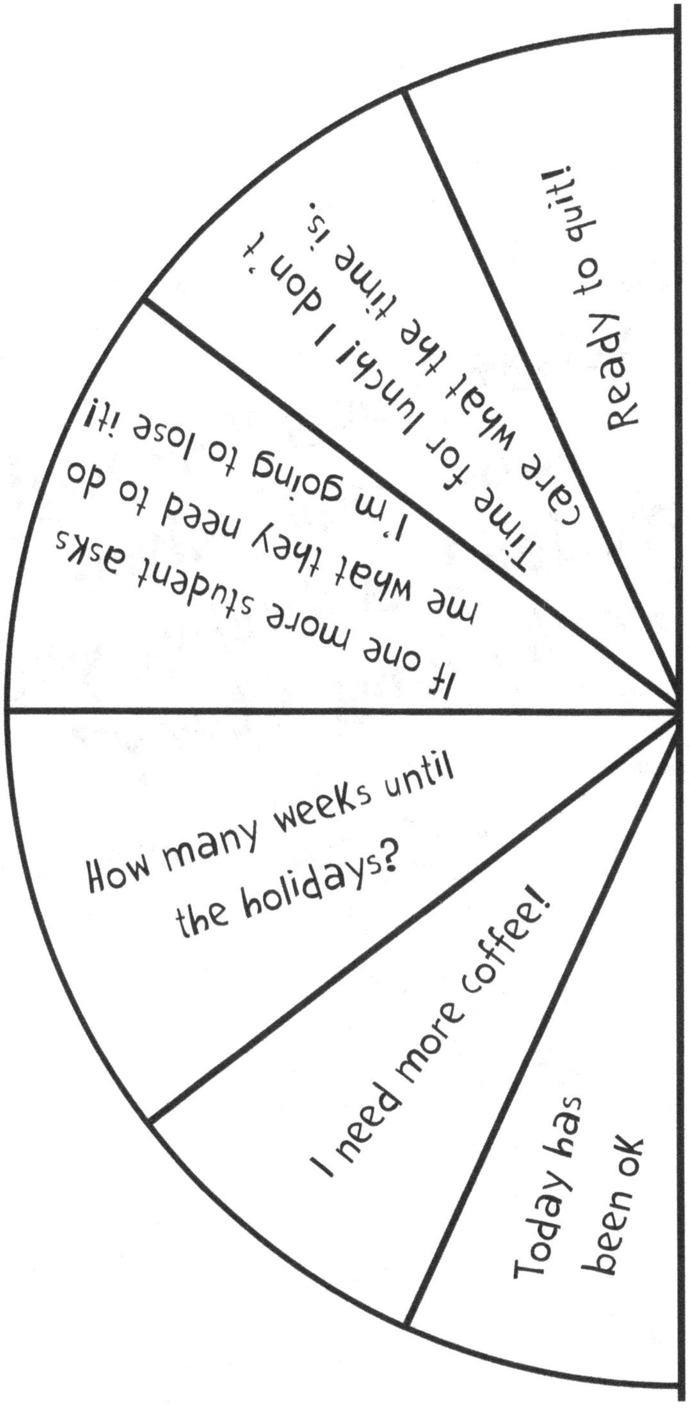

Ready to quit!

Time for lunch! I don't care what the time is.

If one more student asks me what they need to do I'm going to lose it!

How many weeks until the holidays?

I need more coffee!

Today has been ok

What goes through your head when a student is telling you a really long story?

WE ALL KNOW TEACHERS LOVE TO MAKE TO-DO LISTS. MAKE A SUMMER HOLIDAY TO-DO LIST

(NO SCHOOL WORK IS ALLOWED!).

Summer to-do list:

To relieve stress:

1. Take a deep breath in

2. Hold this book tight in your hands

3. Now throw it at the wall

4. Repeat steps 1—3 for as long as needed.

PAINT AN IMAGE WITH COFFEE.

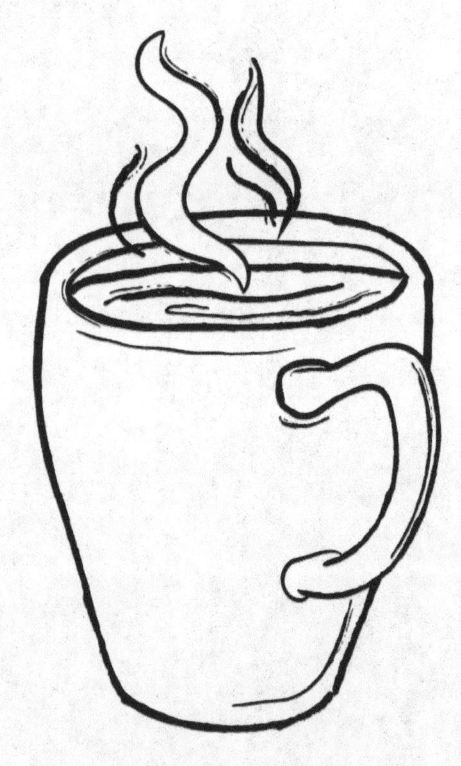

CHEW GUM ALL DAY.

TALLY HOW MANY STUDENTS NOTICE AND TELL YOU TO SPIT IT OUT.

Using your favourite teacher
pen, write yourself a little
comment on how great you're
doing today!

Write down your favourite and cringiest teacher phrases.

For example "The bell doesn't dismiss you. I dismiss you!"

List ten things you'd like to do before your next birthday.

1.

2.

3.

4.

5.

6.

7.

8.

9.

10.

WRITE OUT THE REPORT
CARD COMMENT YOU
WISH YOU COULD SEND
HOME TO PARENTS.

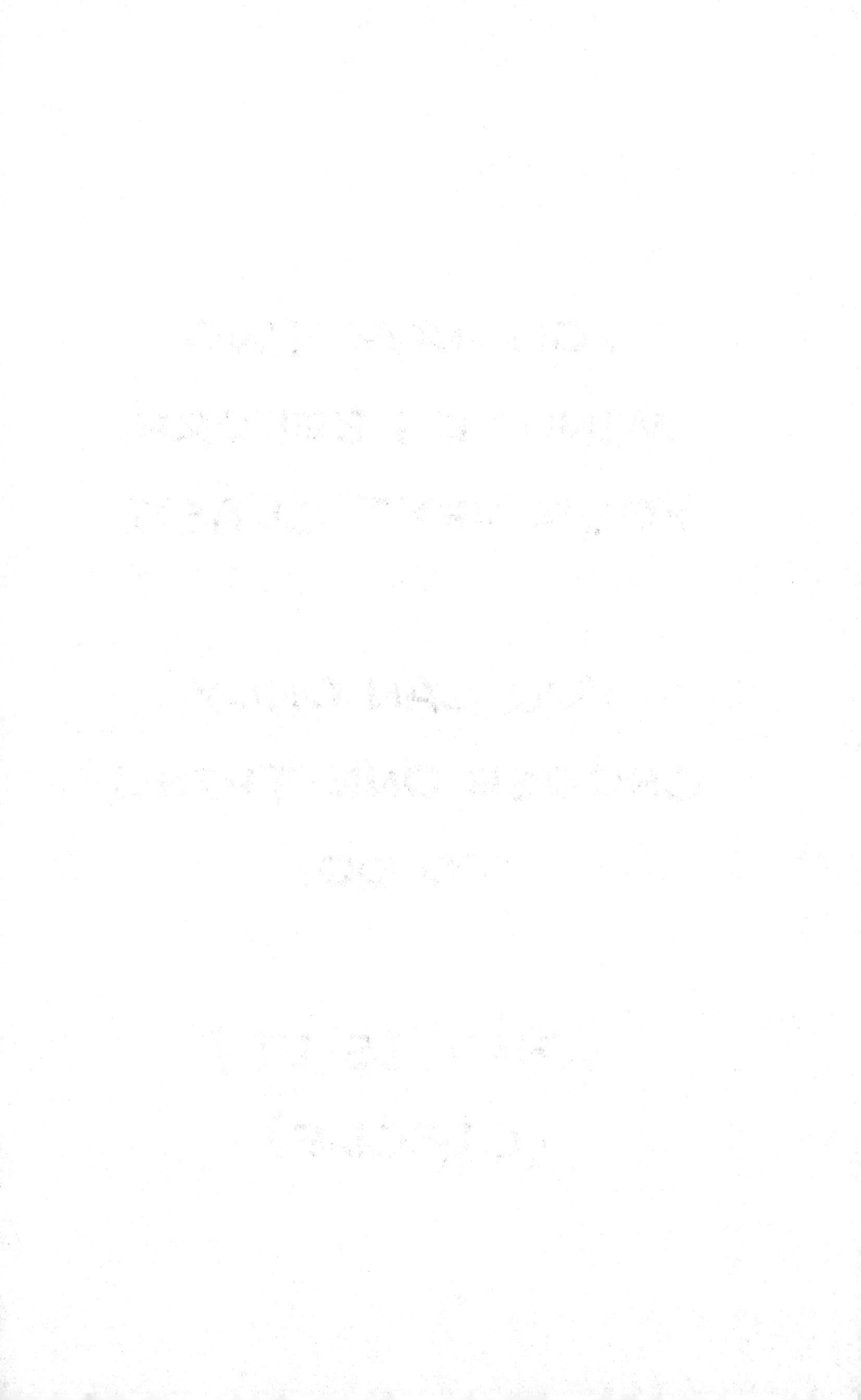

YOU HAVE TWO
MINUTES BEFORE
YOUR NEXT CLASS.

YOU CAN ONLY
CHOOSE ONE THING
TO DO.

WHAT IS IT?
(CIRCLE)

Go to the toilet.

Make a coffee.

Photocopy
resources for your
next lesson.

Have something to eat.

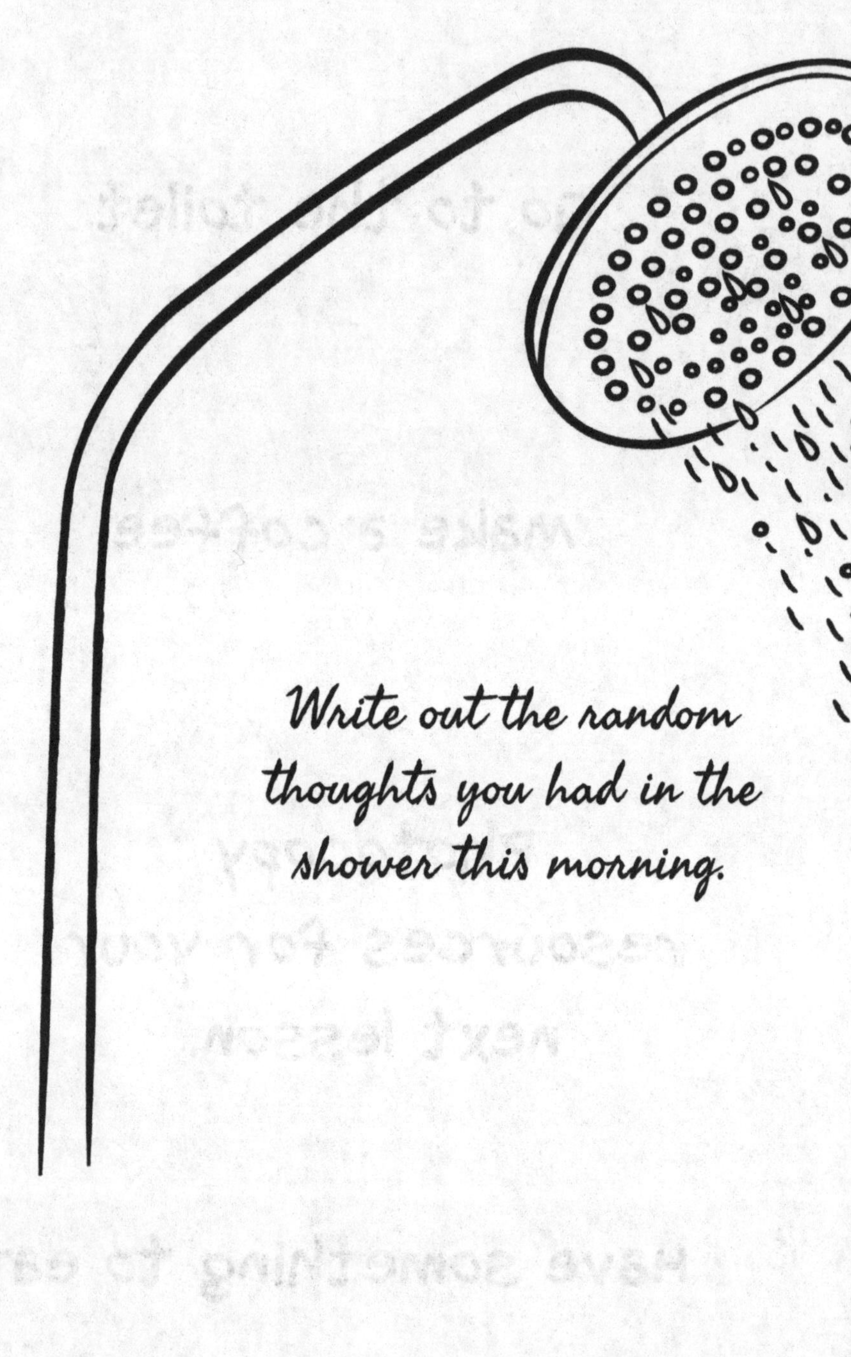

Write out the random
thoughts you had in the
shower this morning.

I'VE HEARD IT ALL!

Circle all the comments you've
heard about your career.

But you get so many holidays!

Kids are so cute.

Don't you finish at 3?

So you pretty much babysit
all day?

Do kids just colour in all day?

They're just Kids! How hard can it be?

Try working with my boss.

I wish I could just play
with Kids all day.

Those who can't, teach, right?

It must be so rewarding
all the time.

What do you
mean you're
burnt out?
They're just Kids.

What paperwork? Don't you just
teach whatever you want?

How long was your
actual break today?

Did you work through
your break today?

YES/NO

IT'S SUNDAY NIGHT.
WHAT DO YOU DO?
(CIRCLE)

GO OUT AND PRETEND
TOMORROW
IS NOT MONDAY.

CHECK YOUR EMAILS.

PREPARE YOUR MEALS
FOR THE WEEK.

PREPARE YOUR
LESSONS FOR
THE WEEK.

ACTUALLY SPEND TIME
WITH YOUR
SIGNIFICANT OTHER.

CRY IN THE CORNER.

COMPLETE THIS TEACHER REPORT CARD.

	Never	Sometimes	Always
I maintain a good work life balance.			
I daydream about changing career paths.			
I am focused during staff meetings.			
I fake laugh at my bosses jokes.			
I work during my lunch break.			
I work on the weekends.			
I complete all my paperwork on time.			
I ask for help when I need it.			
I am kind to myself.			

Positive achievements	
Areas to improve	

TRUE OR

I have put on a movie to avoid teaching.

True/False

I have eaten another staff member's lunch

True/False

I have been hungover at work.

True/False

I have fallen asleep at work.

True/False

FALSE

I have made up my entire lesson plan on the spot.

True/False

I have avoided a parent by hiding somewhere in my school/ classroom

True/False

I have looked up other career options at work

True/False

I have lied on my resume

True/False

WOULD YOU RATHER...
(CIRCLE)

TEACH MATH ALL DAY OR
ENGLISH ALL DAY?

GET MORE PAY BUT FEWER SCHOOL
HOLIDAYS, OR LESS PAY BUT
MORE HOLIDAYS?

START YOUR SCHOOL DAY
EARLIER OR LATER?

HAVE YOUR PRINCIPAL WATCH YOU TEACH
ALL DAY OR HAVE A PARENT WATCH?

WRITE LESSON PLANS ALL DAY BUT
NEVER TEACH THEM OR TEACH ALL DAY
WITH NO LESSON PLAN?

GO ALL DAY WITH NO COFFEE OR
GO ALL DAY WITH NO FOOD?

Trace the lines.

Breathe in as you go over a straight line and breathe out when you go over a curved line.

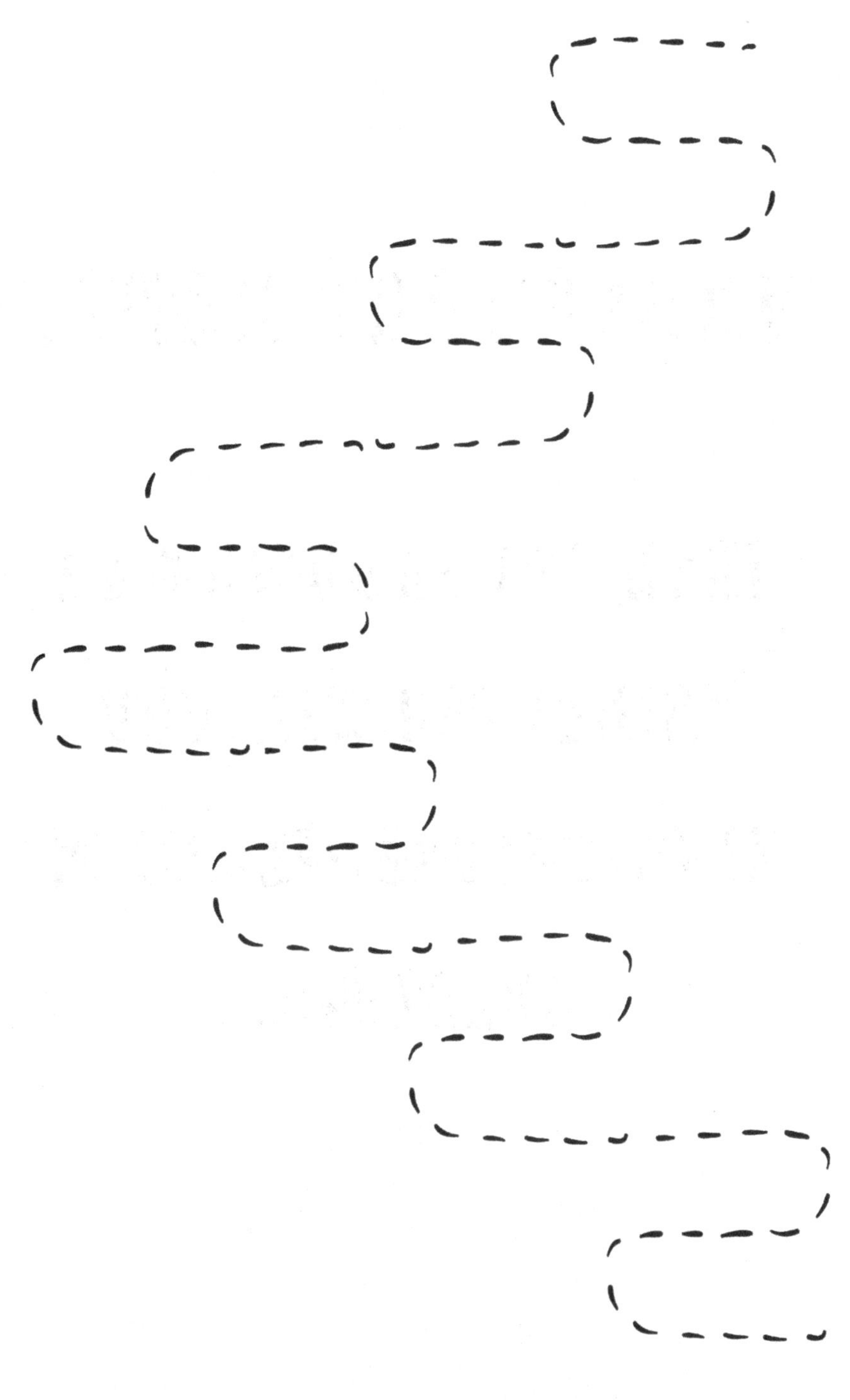

TRACE YOUR HAND.

THEN, WRITE DOWN FIVE THINGS YOU WISH YOU KNEW BEFORE BECOMING A TEACHER.

IF SALLY HAD 3 LOLLIES AND SARAH HAD 2, HOW LONG WOULD IT TAKE FOR THEM TO BE BOUNCING OFF THE WALLS?

DRAW WHAT IT WOULD LOOK LIKE.

IF SALLY HAD 3 LOLLIES
AND SARAH HAD 2, HOW
LONG WOULD IT TAKE FOR
THEM TO BE BOUNCING
OFF THE WALLS?

DRAW WHAT IT WOULD
LOOK LIKE.

AGGRESSIVELY
COVER THESE
PAGES IN STAMPS.

Write an <u>accurate</u> job
description
for your position.

Draw yourself
as a superhero.

what are your
powers?

Draw yourself
as a superhero.

What are your
powers?

Tear this page out in front of your students.

Document their reaction.

DRAW ALL OVER THIS PAGE

DURING A STAFF MEETING

THAT DEFINITELY COULD'VE

BEEN AN EMAIL.

DRAW YOUR GO-TO TEACHER OUTFIT.

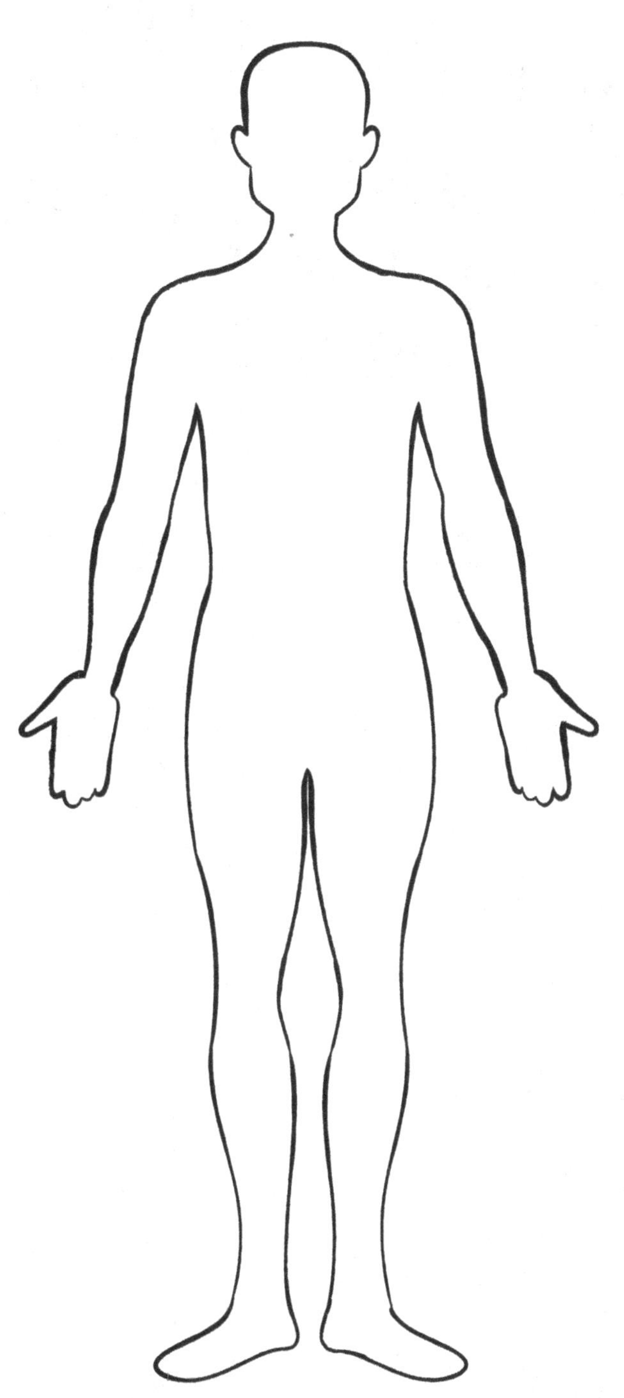

WHAT ARE SOME LIES ABOUT EDUCATION THAT WE SHOULD TALK MORE ABOUT?

WRITE ABOUT YOUR LEAST
FAVOURITE TEACHER WHEN
YOU WERE IN SCHOOL.

WHY DIDN'T YOU LIKE
THEM?

connect the dots.

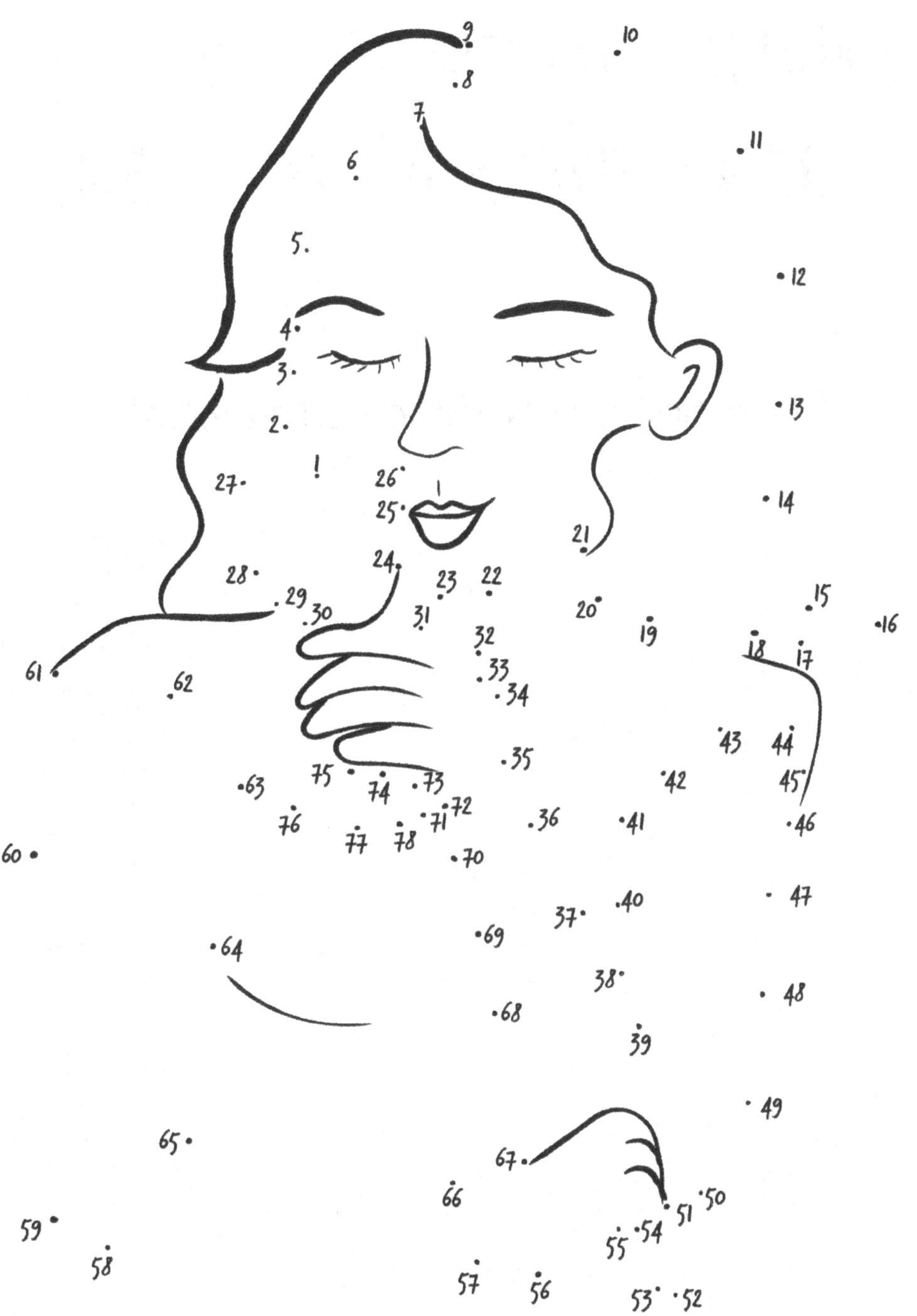

WRITE OUT THIS LINE AS MANY TIMES AS YOU CAN,

"I can not throw things at students".

Complete
the acrostic
poem.

UNDERPAID

Write a method on how to fake confidence in front of students. I've started for you.

step 1: stand up straight, shoulders back

DRAW A PICTURE OF
WHERE YOU'D RATHER
BE RIGHT NOW.

WRITE YOURSELF A
SELF-CARE PLAN

SCAN ME